UNDERSTANDING POINTS

A Caveman's Guide to Happiness

RJ BERGSTROM

PAGE PUBLISHING, INC.
Conneaut Lake, PA

First originally published by Page Publishing 2020

ISBN 978-1-64701-099-7 (pbk)
ISBN 978-1-64701-102-4 (digital)

Printed in the United States of America

Understanding Points
A Caveman's Guide to Happiness

Outline: Understanding Points—learning how to create the best world for you and the people in your life

FOREWORD

Here is the question, "Can we be happy if our partner is not, and can our partner be happy if we are not?"

For some reason, and for all time, people have known that there is something between people; it can be men and women, or any arrangement that you find yourself in, that recognizes both good and bad, or positive and negative things in a relationship. We almost instinctively know that there really are "points" that are a part of every relationship. We earn or are awarded "points" when they are positive and lose "points" when they are negative. Where does this come from, and is this something we can both understand and make a better life for us and the people we care about? To do this, somewhere, sometime way back, someone figured it out and found happiness, and isn't that why we are here?

Are "Points" going to improve all relationships? No. Relationships that have fundamental problems, unresolvable issues, or a lack of trust and mutual respect, are probably not savable. Where these don't exist, and both Partners "Want-To", and honesty and trust are the basis of their relationship, can it be improved and produce a life of Love, Joy and Fulfillment?

The answer is yes, and now we know why. We have discovered that this ancient knowledge predates even written language and was found on the walls of a cavern. Difficult to interpret initially, but the simplicity and truth are apparent when we can finally embrace, that POINTS ARE REAL, and UNDERSTANDING POINTS can help us, and the people we care about, to find happiness.

Our Journey for Truth Begins

A young anthropologist named Peter was part of a team that was in central Turkey, exploring one of the most important discoveries in all of archeology. It was pre-agriculture, yet it contained examples of human artifacts long thought beyond the skills of these ancient ancestors. Two hundred stone pillars and clues of the twenty large structures they supported told a story of a people that were believed to only be tribal and could not be so communal. Yet here it was, the discovery of Göbekli Tepe.

Peter was finishing his three week-tour and decided to take a last look around before the noon departure. He took one of the jeeps to the nearby hills lying to the south. Parking on the east side, he stepped out toward the hill as the sun was climbing behind him. Looking back toward the settlement, Peter wondered how long ago one of his ancestors stood in just this spot and what his life was like.

Grabbing his tool bag, Peter turned to walk toward the hills, intending to climb to a better view of the nearby site. As he looked up, he saw the sun was now illuminating an opening. He climbed quickly, concerned the moving sun would take away its guiding light. Peter approached the doorway just as the sun moved above. Pulling out his flashlight, and after a brief pause, he entered the small cavern, possibly as the first visitor in nearly ten thousand years.

Team

Aggie: administrator, career historian, early forties, most people would say was attractive and professional; controlling and smart but pessimistic and grouchy, she was very focused on the money as she is in charge, expectations for valuable results, the business piece of these activities; marriage was dissolving; no children; partner is Dave.

Peter: field archeologist/anthropologist; quiet, passionate scientist; early thirties, tall, dark hair, but slight build; skeptical by nature; generally listens first and then gets into the conversation; married for just a few years, no children yet, not going well; partner is Jasmine.

Mary: archeologist assistant; thoughtful and positive; middle thirties, high energy, always sees bright side; happily married; young children in school; former psychologist; partner is Alex.

Jack: anthropologist with a strong reputation for important discovery; early fifties, big guy, very smart, thoughtful, polite, but very funny; happily married; children out of college; partner is Amy.

The Mission Begins

Aggie Denton, head administrator of the anthropology department of the Smithsonian National Museum of Natural History, sitting alone in her Washington, D.C. office, was finishing a phone call from her attorney, Bill Dewey, of the law firm, Dewey, Cheatum, and Howe. Aggie was going through divorce with her husband of fifteen years.

"You've got to be kidding, Bill. That bastard wants half my 401K *and* alimony?" She listened as he explained how community property worked and how her success was benefiting her husband's position. "I'm sorry, but I have to think about this, Bill. We've been married for fifteen years, and I know we've gone separate ways, but I have to get my head around this attitude. Tell me this, Bill, why are men interested in only one thing?"

Bill thought to himself, *Aggie, maybe you should be more interested in that one thing,* but decided to keep the thought to himself and asked, "Aggie, do you know why divorce is so expensive? Because it's worth it!"

Aggie paused and then responded, "I guess, but I'm torn for lots of reasons. Let me think about this, and I'll call you the first of next week. I have to tell you that I feel there has to be a better ending to this. The last thing I want to do is hurt Dave, but it's still on the list. Thanks for your time, even though I know I'm paying for it. Goodbye, Bill."

Alone in her office, Aggie reflected on the early years with Dave and wished she could go back to those wonderful days. Suddenly there was a knock on the door.

"Yes, come in," responded Aggie.

In walked Peter, an assistant director of the field explorations division of the museum, who appeared very excited about their recent discovery, more so than Aggie had ever seen him.

"Aggie! I mean, Professor Denton, we've found something, something very important. It's some messages from an ancestor that I can't understand, but I think it's the most amazing thing, I...I...I just don't know how to explain it, but you must come to see it!"

"Peter, I've got a lot of things going on here, so I'm not really interested in more on my desk right now! But I'll listen, so calm down and tell me about this new find. What did you find, and where is it?"

Peter took a breath and finally sat down. "Okay, as you know, we were on the hills northeast of Sanliurfa, Turkey. Yes, it is near the site of Göbekli Tepe. I was there when I found the entrance to a cave we just never saw before, Aggie. I went in, and with my lantern, I saw the drawings. The drawings, Aggie, are from around 8000 BC, or even earlier. But they are so well preserved you can see everything. It looks like someone left us a story of some kind. We need to get you there so we can understand it."

"Okay, Peter, you know that I'm a tough sell, especially when you're asking for another expensive project. But I respect your experience, so I might go along, but I want to keep it small. The discovery of that site is so fantastic, and I knew Professor Klaus Schmidt when he announced the find in 1995. I don't have much left to spend on this, but anything connected to this site is, without question, something we need to do! So let's have a small team and make it quick. I don't want to take more than a week or so. You can handle all of the digging and organizing, but we will need some help. Who else should we think about inviting?"

"Well, Mary for sure. She's been with me for over two years now and is really invaluable. She is great on every team that I've had her on, and I think you will appreciate her and her attitude. She has a couple of young kids and doesn't like to be gone as much now, but she's the best. I follow her on Facebook and was hoping you would approve. She said she is available. I'd like to commit to her if that's okay with you?" Peter liked that he could work with Mary again.

Aggie generally liked to have teams that enjoyed working together.

"Sounds like a good pick if you really think so. I also think we need the best anthropologist we can find. What do you think about Jack?"

"Yes, I think he's the right guy. He did the best work when we were trying to translate the hieroglyphics we found in that early Egyptian tomb. He was the one who finally interpreted and understood the symbols before anyone. Yeah, Jack is the guy, Aggie."

"I have to tell you, Peter, that you are coming to me at an interesting time." She paused to consider the demands of an expedition, her personal situation, and where it will all lead. "So let's do it. I will arrange flights, so let's plan on everyone getting to Ankara by the fifteenth, and that gives us two weeks. Can you have everything ready to go by then?"

"Yes, ma'am, and I think you are making a very good decision. I will say that in my fifteen years of digging into the past, from what I've seen, this could be the biggest find of our careers."

"Peter, I hope you're right. I'm ready for something positive in my life."

Aggie shook Peter's hand, and he left.

Aggie coordinated the group logistics, and the plans were in place to arrive in Turkey on the fifteenth.

The Advance Team Prepares

Jack and Peter arrived a day early as planned to assemble the equipment for the expedition. They met with the local contacts, put together the arrangements for vehicles, and agreed to end the day with drinks and dinner before Aggie and Mary joined them the next day. The Raymar Hotel restaurant was very Arabic, modern, and comfortable. Jack and Peter appreciated the history of the location and smiled as they arrived and were guided to a table by the entrance so they could watch and be close to the passersby. They were ending a hard day and ready to relax.

Peter was pleased with the results and was really excited about the next few days of exploration.

"Jack, we are going to have a fantastic adventure here. I hope you are feeling good about everything?"

Before Jack could answer, a waiter arrived at the tableside and, with a smile, asked if they would like a drink.

"Well, thank you, and yes, we would. Can I ask your first name?"

Our waiter stood straight up and answered, "Yes, sir, my name is Wasim. I am pleased to help you."

Jack looked at Wasim and smiled back. "I think that means handsome, doesn't it?"

Their waiter smiled back and said, "Why, yes, sir, it does. You are the first non-Arabic to know that, and may I ask, do you know where it comes from?"

Jack was pleased that he knew a little bit of our waiter's origin.

"I'm sorry, but I don't. I think that maybe it is from an Israeli reference. Could that be?"

Wasim leaned toward Jack and quietly confirmed his speculation, "Yes, sir, it is. Our people have been here for many, many years, and we live here in peace, but we do not show ourselves. I appreciate your knowledge very much. What can I bring you so you might enjoy your evening?"

Jack looked at Wasim with understanding.

"A couple of beers would be just fine. Is that okay, Peter?" asked Jack.

Peter had enjoyed this exchange. "Sure, a beer sounds great. Thanks, Wasim." Wasim smiled again and left. "Jack, what was that about? Do you do that everywhere you go?"

Jack explained, "I don't know, Peter. I learned a long time ago the people that are in front us are important, and if I take the time to learn their name, it is a gesture of appreciation. Wasn't it interesting what we learned in just a few minutes and how he reacted to my questions? To answer your question, yes, I try to ask for their first name only because I respect that they are doing something for me."

"Well, I just learned something, and I like it. Thanks, Jack! Now, about the expedition, that was a lot of work, and I hope I have all of the equipment we are going to need. The carbon-dating equipment, recorders, and the cameras are all here. I'm ready for a breakthrough experience because that's what I think we have here."

Jack was happy to agree, "I really am, Peter, and I think you have done a great job of laying the groundwork for this and what could be a significant discovery for all of us. You have come a long way from the young intern I met not that many years ago. What have you been doing since then?"

Peter was pleased to update Jack, whom he has respected since first meeting just ten years earlier.

"Well, Jack, I finished my bachelor degree in history, spent some time at the National Anthropology Museum in Mexico, grabbed my Master's degree, and married a girl from the West Coast, and I'm trying to figure things out. How about you? The last time we were together, you had a couple of young kids, and you were constantly calling home about soccer games and dance recitals. Is all that family stuff still going well?"

Jack smiled and answered, "Yes, and everything is very good, but it's always what you make it. Sounds like you've done just what I thought you would. You're doing well. How does your wife feel about you doing these trips?"

Peter took a moment to consider his answer. "Well, I thought I married Miss Right. I just didn't know her first name was Always."

Jack laughed and asked, "So, how long have you been together?"

"I've known Jasmine for almost nine years and married for six. It is a struggle. I just wish I could disable the 'autocorrect function' she has on everything I do and say. I mean, I try to compromise, and that seems to mean that I admit I'm wrong, and then she agrees with me. Jack, I should have known we were going to have trouble. After all, I'm a Libra, and she's a bitch. Is that the way things go, Jack? I know that marriage is an institution, but I don't think I want to live in an institution."

Jack was listening and wanted to be supportive of Peter's issues.

"I'm not sure if this helps, but many people think love is blind, and marriage is an eye-opener. Lots of guys think marriage is a give-and-take arrangement—husband gives, and the wife takes. I'm sorry, but I don't see it that way at all."

Peter had now had a few drinks and continued with, "What I've seen of marriage so far, Jack, is that it is a process. A process of finding out what kind of a man your wife would have preferred. It's like love is one long, sweet dream, and marriage is the alarm clock."

Not wanting to say the wrong thing, Jack hesitated and said, "Peter, sounds like things could be better. I have to tell you that I have the greatest life because of my relationship with my wife. I don't know if I'm just lucky, or if there is something I've learned. I hope you figure it out and have what I have."

Peter ended the conversation with, "So far, Jack, I've learned what the difference is between a girlfriend and a wife. About thirty pounds."

They both laughed and called it a night.

The Balance of the Team Depart

Arriving at the gate for the flight to Ankara, Aggie found Mary was already waiting.

Smiling as she approached, she said, "Mary, how nice to see you and I'm really pleased you can join our expedition. You look great, what's new, and how have you been?"

Mary stood and gave Aggie a hug.

"I'm good, Aggie, and it's wonderful to see you! I was so excited when Peter told me I was being considered for this expedition. I've learned so much the last few years since I last worked for you. I've been in some fantastic digs and can't wait to get to the site for this adventure! Peter has really sold me on this discovery."

"Me too, Mary," shared Aggie as they sat down together near the gate. "Peter has been very convincing. He and Jack arrived earlier today and have all the arrangements in place for us to get right to the site and get to work. I think I heard that you've had a couple of children, and your family is getting busy. Do I have that right?"

"You do, Aggie, I've been married for six years now, and our children, a four-year-old daughter and a one-year-old son, are keeping us very busy and happy. How about you, Aggie?"

"I'm happy for you, Mary. Well, we were happy for a few years when we were first married fifteen years ago, but it has been falling apart for the last seven or eight. I'm afraid we are divorcing soon, and I'm getting the short end of the stick. I think he is just like most guys. It's the difference between men and dogs. After the first year, the dog is still excited to see you."

Mary didn't know where to go to be supportive, so she said, "You're right, Aggie, guys can be a little primitive in their behavior. I think their inner caveman takes control more often than they think."

"How about most of the time, Mary!" Aggie caught her breath. "In the beginning, we both thought it was 'love at first sight,' but now I think that just saves guys a lot of time. I'm realizing women can fake an orgasm, but men can fake a whole relationship. I guess there's nothing left to care about."

"I'm so sorry to hear that, Aggie." Mary thought about how happy she was. "Is there a chance you two could work things out?"

"I wanted to, but our last argument did not go well. I asked him, 'Are you ignorant or just apathetic?' and he said, 'I don't know, and I don't care.' That was where it ended."

Mary reluctantly smiled with her acceptance.

Trying to appear in agreement, Mary said, "I know, Aggie. Do you know what the difference is between a boyfriend and a husband? About thirty minutes."

They both laughed and boarded the flight to Ankara Turkey.

The Team Gathers

After confirming everyone arrived safely, Aggie invited the team to dinner. Aggie, Peter, Mary, and Jack had their first conversation.

They met in the hotel restaurant. Aggie, already seated at the table when Jack arrived, stood to greet him.

"Aggie, it's great to see you again. I think it's been about ten years, and you have to tell me something. How come I'm getting older, and you're not?"

Smiling, Aggie gave Jack a hug and said, "I know BS when I hear it, Jack, but thank you. I'm glad you're here."

Aggie welcomed everyone, and they settled into a pre-departure meal.

"I appreciate everyone's sacrifice to be here and to bring your talents to the project. I'm excited as well to be here, and probably like you, I want to find something that matters, that is a significant message, and that is what Peter has convinced me is here waiting for us."

Jack patted Peter on the back.

Aggie continued, "As you all know, the discovery at Göbekli Tepe has changed many of the theories of the development of our earliest ancestors. The site is pre-pottery, Neolithic, and pre-metallurgy. It predates the Stonehenge ruins by five thousand years and the Egyptian pyramids by six thousand years. The settlement includes fantastic stone columns, carved, moved, and erected even before agriculture was developed. To now learn that Peter has found drawings left by these same people could be the highlight of our careers. I think everyone knows Jack either from the past or reputation. Glad you're here. Have you been to the site, Jack?"

"I have, Aggie, and I agree that what we have found there changed the world of anthropology. I know that we have found drawings all over the world, and many far older than what we are headed toward. To know there are drawings from these same people is incredible. What these people left is so much more than we expected from this era of human evolution. I can't wait to get there, Aggie, and appreciate you inviting me here."

"I appreciate you being here, Jack. And Mary, while I've known you for quite some time, we haven't worked together for years. Peter convinced me you are a very good addition to our little team. So I will turn this over to Peter, the explorer that found the drawings. Peter?"

"Thanks, Aggie. I'm not sure what you all will think, but there is something different here. It is not like anything I've ever seen. I will tell you this: there is something here that is a message. What's different and why I think you, Jack, are the right expert to interpret the drawings we found. They're not symbols like we've seen around the world, more like pictographs. At first, I thought they are just random, but I think there is an important set of messages. We have a very big day tomorrow."

Aggie agreed, "Thanks, Peter and Jack. Now we need to get to sleep as we need to be there on time. From what Peter has told me, we need to be in position at the right time, and to do that, we need to leave early. We have a 4:00a.m. departure. I can't wait to see you all in the morning."

They called it a night, and all headed to their rooms. All needed to be up early and ready for the expedition.

The Expedition Begins: Vehicle One

They boarded their Land Rovers and headed into the desert. Aggie was riding with Jack, and Mary with Peter in the lead vehicle. It's pre-dawn as they departed Ankara for the adventure of their lives.

Mary used the opportunity to thank Peter.

"I really appreciate you supporting me for this project, Peter. It was very exciting to get that phone call. And we have two of the best to work with, Aggie and Jack. This should be a very important expedition. Aggie and I had a good visit at the airport, and I know she is happy to be here. I'm sure she is glad to be out of the office and back in the field. I was disappointed to hear she is going through a divorce. I think she's glad to be gone."

"Well, I'm glad you're here, and you deserve to be. As far as Aggie goes, I can relate to her situation. I don't know for sure, but I may be close to that same process. I'm also okay being gone for a while. We just don't seem to be communicating very well. I can't understand some of the things she says and what she means."

Now Mary was feeling uncomfortable with another personal issue she really didn't want to know about.

"Communication can be hard work sometimes, Peter. It takes some time to figure out. I've been married a little longer than you I think, and conversations get better, but you do have to work at it."

"Now, that is the challenge, and I'm starting to learn. Here's an example. If she says, 'I'm okay,' then I think she's fine. When she says, 'I'm fine,' well, now I know she's not okay. It took me years to learn that. There should be a *man*-ual for guys, don't you think?"

Mary laughed and tried again, "Peter, I think most guys would agree. Getting some help with communicating with their partner could be a really big idea."

Peter focused on the road, considering Mary's comment.

"I get it, Mary. I just learn everything the hard way. I just wish I could tell the difference between a smile and a warning. I also learned that 'What?' doesn't mean she needs clarification. It means she's giving me a chance to change my answer. I need that man-ual!"

Mary thought about where to take this.

"That's a good one, Peter. I know what you mean," she added with a smile. "There's got to be a lot of good stuff between you two, isn't there?"

"There was in the beginning, Mary, but not so much anymore. Jasmine doesn't seem to support me. It's all about her. I think I'm giving 50 percent, maybe more, but I don't think she is." Peter paused then added, "We just don't seem happy?"

Mary considered Peter's comment and said, "Peter, I was taught that happiness is a decision, and I believe that."

"Come on, Mary," said Peter, not accepting her premise. "It can't be that easy."

"I didn't says it's easy, Peter. Let me ask you, do you know people that have lots to be happy about, and they are not? And do you know people that don't have much, and they are happy? I know it's not about stuff, but what is it then?"

Peter considered the question.

"I don't know, Mary. I really wish I did."

The Expedition Begins: Vehicle Two

Meanwhile, Jack and Aggie were following close behind in the second Land Rover. They're discussing the expedition, and Jack shared his enthusiasm.

"You know, Aggie, I always get excited as I get close to the new dig site. It's been several months since I've had a chance to be in the field. How long has it been for you?"

"Way too long, Jack, and I agree. It's great to be out here. I've been the head of the department for over five years, and I'm getting tired of the desk-job thing. I thought I was done with this dirty field work, but I really miss it. Maybe the whole people management thing is what I'm really bored with. I don't know why everyone thinks it's my job to help them with their personal problems, but that's what ends up in my office. Like I don't have problems of my own!"

"I guess that comes with the 'boss thing' and why you get the 'big money', right, Aggie?" replied Jack. "I'm sure you know by now that you have to push back and help them understand how to manage themselves and to leave it at home!"

"Yes, I know they are leaning on me, and I need to put the brakes on that. I think if I started exposing my personal issues, they would run for the hills. In fact, I should do that. I'll dump on them what a destroyed marriage does to you. In the beginning, Jack, time stood still, and now it's—where does the time go?"

Jack didn't know why Aggie was wanting to talk about her personal situation, but wanted to let her open up. "Aggie, I'm really sorry to hear that. What are you going through?"

Aggie realized how much she'd thrown out there.

"No, don't be sorry. I'm sorry, Jack. I don't know why I just did that to you. I feel terrible. Yes, I'm going through a divorce, and I don't know how it happened or why he changed so much. I won't do that to you again. Now, I know if you can't say anything nice, say it to your husband. He's not listening anyway."

Jack knew it was time to change the subject, but couldn't think of one.

"Well, Aggie, maybe this is a good time to be here."

Arrival

After a dusty, six-hour journey, they arrived at the site. Göbekli Tepe was discovered less than twenty-five years earlier, was much, much older than Stonehenge and fifty times larger. Only a small portion of the area had been excavated, but what had been exposed was extremely sophisticated when understood. Our team was not here to explore these remains, but just the discovery Peter made during his time here just three weeks ago. Peter drove to the area close to the bluffs where they parked and prepared for the day.

Unloading all the equipment and the team now facing the side of the hill, Peter explained what they were looking at.

"You probably have the same impression that I had when I first stood here and looked at the hills in front of us. Nothing there but a rocky set of mounds, right? Well, I was here to see the site from a more-distant vantage point and almost moved on, but something made me look closer. So please follow me."

They followed Peter toward the southern end of the hills until he stopped them and pointed to a small, dark spot about forty feet up the hill. He looked at his watch and then at the sun.

"We are almost on time, just a few minutes early."

Peter looked again at the sun as it climbed closer to the noon position and back at the hill. After just a few moments Peter pointed to a dark place in the rocks and waited as everyone watched. Then it finally happened. The morning sun entered the dark space between several large boulders and lighted the opening for all to see. The explorers saw the opening, an entry into the hill that looked like a welcoming door to the chamber waiting for them all.

"Okay, everyone, it's time! Let's head up there, and I think you will be amazed at what we are about to learn together," said Peter with a very excited smile. He headed up the hill, and the team picked up the gear for the adventure of their lives.

Peter stopped at the entrance, an opening roughly ten square feet. He turned and smiled at his colleagues. He stooped and entered the dark doorway. Aggie, Jack, and Mary shared excited expressions and followed.

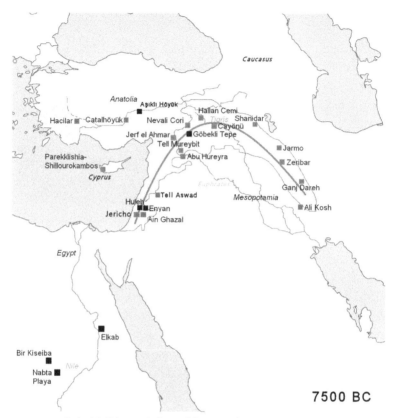

Gobekli Tepe—The Oldest Settlement in History

Gobekli Tepe—A Portion of the Discovery

The Key to Happiness, Understanding Points

Drawing is of man with arrows/spears pointing up and down. The man is looking down with the spears pointing down and up with the spears pointing up.

Peter shone the light on the first drawing and stood back so the rest of the team could all see the drawings that went on deep into the cavern. They all absorbed the drawing, and finally, Aggie tried to interpret the message.

"Peter, since they go from here, and you've seen them, do you think there is a sequence or a story the messages are intending to present? If there is some kind of theme here, perhaps the foundation is here at the beginning. We apparently have a man that is looking at what looks like arrows or spears that are either pointing up or down. Look at how he is looking at the spears. He is looking up at the arrows pointing up and down at the arrows pointing down."

Everyone was quiet and staring, considering the images. Finally, Jack tried to interpret.

"We know that early man uses pictures as there is no written language. All the drawings here, though, are before the pictographs and hieroglyphics we have found all over the world. I think this is the first drawing I've seen that is not connected to a spoken language like the hieroglyphics. Maybe what our messenger is telling us is about how he is looking at the spears or arrows? How do we translate this?"

Mary had an idea. "Could he be a warrior, and he is showing off his arsenal for either hunting or battle, or maybe he is counting his kills? But why are some pointing up, and others down?"

After a pause for considering the question, Peter finally shared his thought, "Could it be that he is telling us that up is positive and down is negative? Maybe this is the key understanding these messages. What do you think this means, Jack?"

"I agree with that, and I wonder, does the number of these 'arrows' mean another part of his message?"

Our team pondered the question.

Mary jumped in, "I think it does. I think that maybe he is counting? You don't see just one, but several! I think he is telling us that it is both what is positive or negative *and* that we need to count the positive and negative. Could that be the message? And where is he going with this? And why are the points between him, and isn't that a woman?"

"It is a woman. He is looking at her, and she at him, so this message is about them. What else could it be?" added Aggie. "And is this really about them? Not a historical event, not a battle, or even a great accomplishment? Could this just be about counting something between this caveman and cavewoman, is that really a message?"

Everyone was quietly considering the message when suddenly Jack burst into a laugh that scared everyone. He laughed until Aggie tried to understand what he was so excited about.

"*Jack*, what the hell is so funny? Tell me, why are you laughing at this?"

Jack was laughing like they had never seen before, and slowly he collected himself.

"I get it. I understand what we are seeing, and it is the most basic, most fundamental thing between people and between us. He is telling us about *points!*"

Mary didn't know what he was talking about. "Points? What are points?"

Jack was still excited and tried to explain, "Okay, let me try to explain it this way. I don't know how to describe what points are. I guess I've always just known. I think guys, could also be girls, naturally 'count' while they do everything. Points are just a way for a guy, or anyone, to keep track of what they are doing. Did they do, or say, something good, or was it bad? That's all I think he is saying to us. I believe guys want to know if they are doing the right thing for their partner, and that is the point!"

"What the hell are you talking about, Jack? Points? What the hell are points?", asked Aggie.

Jack sat down and motioned for Aggie to join him.

"Aggie, let me ask you this. Do you think that sometimes guys do smart things to their partner, and sometimes they do dumb things?"

Aggie nodded in agreement, and Jack continued, "Would you say that the good or smart things are positive, and the dumb things are negative?" Aggie agreed again, and Jack added, "Do you think women spend more time wondering what men are thinking than men actually spend thinking?"

Both Mary and Aggie were shaking their heads yes.

Jack smiled and continued, "Well, there you go! Guys want to do the right things, but it's hard to figure out what the right things are. Aren't we all pretty close to being 'cavemen' when you get down to it? And doesn't it make sense that if we keep track of the right and wrong things, the good and bad, that we will learn what is positive and negative, and if we try to do more smart things than dumb, isn't that better for both?"

Peter had been listening and was anxious to ask, "Jack, you sound just like my dad! He even called them points! Please don't tell me that this is where it started, and my dad knew all this 'stuff'! I'm sorry, but that is unacceptable. I have never had any points in my relationship, but I can think of a lot more negatives than positives if that's where you want to take this "point" thing. I'll give you an example. My wife and I always compromise. I admit I'm wrong, and she agrees with me! Now, where is the positive in that?"

Jack smiled and added, "I don't have the answer to that, Peter, and you have some relationship communication issues to work out. But let me ask you this. Do you still love your wife?"

Peter pondered for just a moment and shared, "I think I do, Jack. I just don't know how to make it the way it should be for both of us."

Jack ended with, "Then you have the 'why' of things figured out. You just need to get to the 'how'."

Our team was silently absorbing the messages. Finally, Aggie began to consider that this was important and a very powerful message for all of us.

"If Jack is right, then I don't know what to think? I've been in archeology for twenty-five years because I wanted to find something important, and this is the bullshit—the simplistic bullshit—that I've been looking for? I think you are reaching here, I mean, really reaching. All I'll give you is that you have *one* possible interpretation. I don't believe it's that simple. I have to see a *lot* more before I'm going to give you that."

Jack calmly smiled at Aggie and stood to reach out and hold her hand.

"Aggie, I've known you a long time, but not very well. I've always thought of you as very smart person, but you need to keep an open mind about this. I've always liked you, but you can be a little closed-minded. I'm guessing it will make more sense as we go on."

Peter had been quiet too long, and it seemed a good time to refocus, "Well, I just don't know where this is going. Why did he put this here, and what is he trying to do? Is this a lesson of some sort, or is he just writing down what he thinks? It can't be that points are that important, enough for him to do all this, are they? And how about this, maybe he is showing there are different ways to kill her? Maybe the easiest way is hold the spears up? Yeah, how about that?"

"I don't know either, Peter. That's just the logical interpretation that occurs to me," shared Jack. "And if I'm right and that is the message, I think we will learn that **The Key to Happiness in Understanding Points**. Let's keep going."

Learning What is Positive & Negative, Smart & Dumb

Our man is looking toward his partner from two positions: one looking down with arrows pointing down at her, the other looking up with the arrows at his partner. This time, however, there is a line through the man looking down.

Now Peter was laughing, "Ha, I was right! This guy has had it with this woman, and now he's trying to figure out which way he should kill her! That makes sense to me because the arrows are all pointing at her, and she probably drove him to it! That's what women do!"

"So it's the women's fault!" barked Aggie. "This caveman, like all men, is abusing this woman. He's probably been beating her, and now he's going to kill her! Even in this prehistoric record, man is abusing woman!"

Mary had been quiet, staring at the wall, and seemed to have a question.

"If that is the message, why is there a line through the down arrows? Is this caveman telling us about his relationship? He is up or positive with the arrows pointing up and negative when they are down. Isn't he telling us what to do and what not to do?"

"That's what I think, Mary," added Jack. "Our man is saying no to the negative and yes to all the positive with his woman. I think it's as simple as that."

Aggie was standing now and wanted to push back.

"Sure, Jack, and Prince Charming isn't a Disney character. He really exists! Give me a break. There is no Prince Charming, at least in the world I've lived in my whole life. I'm starting to think this is not anything but fiction! If you are, then I'm not buying it. That is way too simple. No way, Jack."

"I'm sorry," Mary said with some reluctance, "but I see that he is telling us to take out the negative and only be positive toward your partner. That makes more sense than anything else. He is all about her, 100 percent. A friend of mine recently said his relationship could be much better, and he thought a fifty-fifty was the right approach, but I don't. And by the way, how could you possibly determine what 50 percent is? I believe your relationship deserves 100 percent from both. That's all you have, and your partner deserves it, don't they?"

Peter recalled their conversation in the Rover, crossing the desert, and considered the message.

"Well, a 100 percent sounds like you give up everything for your 'partner.' I still think he wants to shoot her, but I will keep an open mind. I do understand that positive is important."

Jack feels compelled to add his interpretation, "all that may be true, but I believe he's saying that only positive is the focus and negative needs to be eliminated, hence the line through the negative. I think he is suggesting we **Learn what is Positive and Negative, Smart and Dumb**, and then we can improve everything.

Having a Positive Point Balance

Drawing of the man with many positive and negative points, but they are combined to indicate they offset each other, and there is either a positive or negative balance.

Peter was again fired up about what this meant.

"Okay, there are ten up or positive arrows, and five down or negative arrows, and five positive at the end. Is he telling us here that there are more positive than negatives, and the balance is positive? So this is primitive math? Is he keeping score?" asked Peter.

Jack laughed again. "When you think about it, isn't this what guys do? He is just trying to keep score. Heck, isn't this where sports came from? Maybe this is where many things started? We keep score to see who wins, right? Doesn't he just wants to *win* with his partner?"

Aggie was shaking her head no, so Jack added, "Doesn't it seem completely natural? This caveman does something positive to this woman, and she rewards him. He likes that, he wants more rewards, so he keeps experimenting with different ways to be rewarded. He also discovers that some things not only don't work, they have to be either undone or replaced with things that do work. Finally, he starts to keep track."

Peter saw it differently and said, "The only one keeping track, Jack, is the woman, and it's only the mistakes she is keeping track of. That's the one thing he *can* count on. So why does he need to keep track when she's doing it for him?"

Mary wants to move on, "If that were the message, Peter, I don't think our messenger would put all of this up here for us. I agree that he wants to *win*, but I see this is a *win-win*. They both win. I think he is just telling us another **Key is to Have a Positive point Balance**. Let's move on, and I think we will see that is what this is."

Points are Earned,
Your Partner Decides

Drawing shows our man surrounded by four different scenes, and each are symbolizing something that our man is doing. The first appears to be a flower, and there is one point alongside, then an animal, and what looks like food with two points, then looks like a hut of some kind with three points. Finally, several small people and four points.

Peter moved the lights to the next illustrations. Our team was silent as they took in the scenes.

Peter had an attitude now.

"Here we go. Here's our guy working his ass off, and she looks down on him like he works for her! That's the real message—that guys are screwed. Their lives are just to please her! Talk about abuse. This guy is a slave!"

Finally, Mary asked the question, "It looks like he is telling us that he earns different numbers of points with each of these examples, but she is looking down on them. Could this mean that each of these things he does, and the points that are there for him, are up to her?"

Jack nodded his head in agreement and said, "I think you're right, Mary. He is doing things for her, but she decides how many points he gets. That explains how he learned that he needed to keep track things that he does and what it does for him. Did any of you read *Women are from Venus and Men are from Mars?* Well, I see it differently. I think women are from Paris, and men are from Chicago. I mean, women and men are wired differently. Women are more emotional, thoughtful, and caring. Men are pragmatic, bottom-line, and look at things logically. We just are different, and guys need help living with these differences. It looks like our caveman has experimented and learned what works and what doesn't, and he's trying to keep track of everything with *points!* And the real game he is playing is that he doesn't get to decide how many or even if he gets any points—she does! And that is why he needs to keep track!" Jack pauses and then adds, "Another way to look at it is, 'beauty is in the eye of the beholder,' Points are awarded by the receiver."

Aggie was getting fired up and said, "Are you kidding me? She gets to decide nothing. She's not a little princess that has this guy 'waiting' on her. She's 'waiting' on him! That's what women do and what men expect them to do, always have, always will. That's the differences in the sexes, and you know it!"

"That's pretty pessimistic, Aggie," shared Jack. "And I know that is how a lot of people see things like relationships, powerful versus weak. But I think our caveman is better than that. He knows and is telling us his life is better, for everyone, when he works at 'winning' with her. He knows he will be happy when she is happy. It's okay that he might see it as a game. Remember, all this is before there were games, and what's wrong with being happy by winning for him and her?"

Aggie didn't agree. "Jack, this is just a different way for a guy to get what he wants, isn't it?"

"Aggie, I think he wants her happy because he knows that will make him happy," added Jack.

"If that's true, Jack, and he really is saying that, then I think we have found an extinct species of man because there aren't any like him today."

Mary's compelled to answer, "I'm glad I don't agree with that, Aggie, and I think it goes both ways. Isn't it true that the same exchange is there for her with him? This isn't a male-to-female issue, it goes female-to-male as well. **Points are Earned, and your Partner decides**. Let's see what's next."

You Have to be Your Best,
to be the Best Partner

Our man in this drawing is the center of the message, and this time the points seem to be inside of him. He is looking up, and then they are outside of him. His partner is also surrounded by points, and she also has points inside of her.

Aggie was becoming a contrarian.

"I get it. He's so sick of trying to figure out these stupid points that he is shooting himself with all the arrows. He wants to end it all and is committing suicide. Ha! That's this message."

"Makes sense to me, Aggie!" declared Peter. "The only problem is how do you shoot yourself with an arrow? This just shows that he wants to if he could!"

Mary saw it differently and said, "Come on, Aggie. You know this is important. I think he is telling us that he needs positive points for himself. The positive points are inside of him and then outside, like he is the source, and the points are coming from him. When I was a psychology student, we learned how important it is to understand the influence of the self-image, and he is telling us that he not only knows that, he is working on it. This is so fascinating if that's what we are looking at."

Peter disagreed, "Self-image—are you kidding me? You're saying this caveman not only knows that he has a self-image, he knows how to improve it? You are nuts. You're reaching for something that is not there."

Mary tried to explain, "I know, Peter, but think about this. He doesn't have *any* other influences on how he thinks, no social media, no news, no politics, no religion, and not even a written language. He is free to think about how things work, the direct cause and effect of everything. Doesn't it make sense that he sees things a lot more clearly than you or I ever could? I think this is a wonderful statement of what life is like when everything is pure! There is no way for us today to replicate what is going on in his mind because we are all polluted with the world around us and the world we've lived in all our lives."

Aggie laughed, "It's you that's polluted, Mary. You have a warm, fuzzy idea of people, and that's not the way it is. People are out for themselves, not about others. Wake up and accept that because that's life."

"I think Mary is on the right track here, everyone", said Jack. "Not only is our messenger displaying his self-awareness, he is showing how to control yourself and improve the world he's in by improving himself. And Mary, it's wonderful you're thinking about how pure his world is. Imagine completely wiping your hard drive clean and how you would look at things. It's a fascinating idea, Mary. I really love it."

Appreciating Jack's support, Mary adds, "And look how his arrows, I mean his points, are elevating his mate. Do you think he is understanding that everything is 'inside out,' in other words, he knows that he needs to be a better man and then he will be a better Partner?

Sensing a disagreement from a couple of his Team members, Jack adds, "Let me put it this way, when I was getting out of college, some classmates were going off to 'find themselves'. They were going to 'backpack' through Europe, or 'backpack' through the Rockies, or work on shrimp boat, or go to the starving areas of Biafra, to 'find themselves'. But there isn't anything to 'find'! Life is about 'Defining' yourself. You decide who you are, not the world. You decide what you are going to do and who you are going to be."

Aggie wants to be a little more of a leader by attempting a summary, "so you're saying **You Have to be Your Best, to be the Best Partner**. I really wish that was how people are". Jack and Mary smile back.

Mary is moved and added, "I have to tell you that is what my husband does for me. Since we met, he has always been my biggest supporter. I was very insecure, but Alex has always been building me up, always with a smile, always helping me understand how good I am and could be. He makes me feel so good!"

Mary was overwhelmed with this sharing, this reflection of what her life was like.

She collected herself and continued, "I don't know how this can be, but this ancient man, this caveman, has sent a message that I, a twenty-first-century woman, am moved by. How can this be?"

Everyone was quiet, allowing Mary's experience to settle and to consider her comments.

Finally, Jack broke the silence, "Mary, I so appreciate you letting us see this through your eyes and your heart. I really can't explain why. I need to sort through this some more, but I get it. I feel like our messenger has put my life up here as well. I love my wife so much, and we have this relationship. She has always believed in me. She gives me courage, especially when I doubt myself. This is a two-way process. I do my best to be her best supporter, but for years I didn't realize she was my inner foundation. I have six books that I've written, and none of them would be out there without Amy."

Again, everyone was silent, trying to absorb all this. Aggie was not so moved.

"So you two got lucky, you two found another sap that surrenders their identity to be your 'Sherpa.' That is not the mainstream reality in life, guys, and I'm not going to let this interpretation of these caveman messages go out like this. How about if the 'arrows' are like little daggers into the heart of each of these people because they are together, and that's what happens when people are together. That's my experience, since that's what we're doing here. Sorry that's so negative, but that's how I see all this."

"Aggie and I are pretty close on this," said Peter. "I don't see the positive in a relationship. There's only one reason people are together, and that's physical. That's the reason I'm married. And all I do is pay for it, and now I'm not even getting that!"

Peter's confession stunned the team, and no one knew where to take this now. Peter felt that was maybe a little too much, so he added, "Okay, let me put it this way, marriage is like coffee. First, it's really hot. Then it's just right. Then it helps you to get off your ass and do things."

Lift Your Partner From the Inside

Our man in this scene seems to be using his positive points to elevate his partner, and his partner is sending them back to him.

Peter was ready to take a shot at the next drawing.

"All right, I want to try this one. So our caveman understands that he can elevate his 'self-image' with positive points. I'm still doubting that, but in this drawing, is he telling us he knows she has a self-image? Rather than doing things for her, is he telling us he is giving her points to elevate her self-image?"

Aggie was getting upset and said, "There isn't a man that has ever made a woman feel better about herself, and that's what you're saying? Every man, at least the ones I've met—and that's quite a few—are not about anything but themselves."

Mary went back to her psychology training. "Aggie, have you ever seen the 'Old Woman, Young Woman' drawing?"

Aggie thought about it and then answered, "Yes, in college. I think it is an old woman looking down, and the same drawing is a young woman looking up and away. Is that the drawing you're talking about?"

Mary smiled and acknowledged Aggie's interpretation, "Very good, Aggie, that's right. Do you remember which of the women you saw first?"

Aggie reflected then added, "That's a long time ago, Mary, but I think I saw the old woman. Then the instructor showed me the young woman. Why on earth are you bringing that up?"

Again, Mary smiled. "The purpose of the drawing is that we all 'lock on and then lock out.' In other words, you saw the 'old woman' and then couldn't see the 'young woman.' Your brain locked out the other point of view. We all do it, Aggie. It's the way our brains work. Could it be that you're just seeing the 'old woman' in these drawings?"

"Mary, I have always thought I had an open mind. You're saying that I am not seeing the real message because I'm locking on the wrong interpretation? I don't think so, but I'll keep an open mind. Let's move on to the next drawing and see what we see."

Peter was seeing it differently and said, "Old woman, young woman, whatever. What I think he is saying is that if you make your partner feel good about themselves, they will want to be with you. Really, is that how easy he is saying this is? So all you have to do is **Lift Your Partner From The Inside**? I thought I was doing that, I have to think about this." Peter pauses, "Okay, let's move on."

Life with Partner, "All-In"

The message includes our man and his partner, and the scene is both having positive points being together. They are both at the same place and looking up.

Peter considered the next message and didn't like what he was seeing.

"So am I seeing what I think I am? Are they both looking up, and everything is the positive arrows or points? Did our prehistoric friend have some drugs, and this is the first 'love in'? I know what this is. It's the very first fairy tale! This is Disney's grandfather times five hundred! So we are supposed to think that he has a life with this woman that is just positive points, and everything is perfect. If that's not a fantasy, I've never heard of one."

"Peter has this one nailed," announced Aggie. "This drawing is a cartoon of what he wants. There is no way this is his life. Men are not about being happy. They are into controlling and self-gratification. I think that all this is our caveman's dream and is in no way his life. Not a chance, no way."

Mary seemed thoughtful on this.

She paused and then added, "I think I know what this is about, and I like it! I think this is my life, I really do! He is showing us that they are together, and it is positive. They are not independent, nor are they dependent. They are interdependent! Isn't that the highest level a relationship can arrive at?"

Jack was starting to see her perspective and said, "When you say interdependent, you mean you are a team, and that is better, so you are better together than apart. Is that what you're saying?"

Mary continued to explain her interpretation of this message, "Yes, Jack, I believe it is. Before I met Alex, I had fun, enjoyed time with friends, liked what I did in my job and the people that I worked with. But then I met Alex, and I knew that he was it, the reason I am here, my life partner. I suppose, from an empirical perspective, you could say we're synergistic. The 'one plus one equals three' equation. I am more with Alex than without. I'm not dependent. I'm more than that. I'm interdependent, and I love it. I would never want my life before. It was just me, yes, some friends, but I have my family, my children, my husband, and there isn't anything else I want. It is so busy, so much to do, and every day is wonderful."

Jack, smiling, added, "Mary, you remind me of Amy and the life we have. The nonstop, young children years go by so fast you won't believe it. We miss them a lot, but we love our lives now and really enjoy being together. It was just like that for us though, and I can't imagine—don't want to imagine—not having our lives that we have had." Speaking from my experience, **Life with my Partner has been "All-In."**

Communication, Starts with Listening

Our messenger has three drawings. The first image is our man and the woman facing each other. It has lots of arrows pointing down and a line through all of it. The second has his hand on the side of his head, and both facing each other. The last looks like our woman with her man inside of her.

Peter was not understanding the drawing.

"What is this a drawing of? The first drawing is all down arrows and has a line through it. They are facing each other, and is he trying to show they are talking? And then is that his hand next to his ear?"

Aggie thought that was hilarious. "Hah, that's it. That is bull-shit! Is this saying this guy, or any guy, is *listening*? Not buying it. I've never met a guy that really listens, not for very long anyway!"

Peter had had it, "So you're saying guys don't listen, but women do? Not in my world. Maybe after I say it two or three times, she might hear me. And then she says I don't listen to her, and that's when the arguments start. A woman has the last word in any argument. Anything a man says after that is the beginning of a new argument."

Mary paused and finally added, "Well, could it be that he is telling us arguing is all negative and that if he is showing us that he is listening, then it is more positive. My dad once told me, 'A wise man once said…nothing. He only listened'."

Mary's comment caused everyone to stop and consider the idea.

Jack seemed connected to this topic and said, "Aggie, let me ask you this. When you are in a conversation, are you really listening, or are you just waiting for your turn to talk? Having spent a lot of time with you over the years, I think it's the latter. I'm not sure if what we are being told here is what Peter has translated, but doesn't it make sense? I've listened to you and have a better understanding of where you are coming from. That helps me talk to you, and we get along fine. But Aggie, do you have any idea where I'm coming from?"

Aggie felt cornered and said, "I know where you're coming from, Jack, because I know where all guys are. Don't deny it, Jack."

Jack paused then added, "And there you go, Aggie. You pre-judge, you don't listen, so why would I talk to you?"

Aggie was getting an attitude "So don't!" She stared at Jack for just a moment and then added, "I'm sorry, Jack. That was an awful thing to say to you, and I didn't mean it." She collected herself. "I think you are just too right, and it makes me embarrassed, and I just didn't realize it. Please forgive me."

Jack, smiling, said, "Aggie, no worries. If I didn't care, I wouldn't have said it. I think you are basically great, but sometimes…Now, let's see what this third message means." Jack turned toward the last of the three drawings, in the lower right. "He is displaying our woman with him inside? Am I saying that right?"

Now Peter was energized. "I know what this means! She has sucked him in! He has lost his soul, and he is gone! That's what women do! There's no other way to interpret that, is there!"

Again Mary thoughtfully moved toward the wall and asked, "Could it be that he is, in a way, inside of her, like he is telling us he is seeing things from her perspective? Yes, I think he is telling us about empathy, I really do."

"Empathy!" exploded Aggie. "You are suggesting a 'caveman' can understand the importance of 'empathy'? That would mean that this ancient 'male' is more 'evolved' than any man I've ever spent time with! No, no way, that would mean that this 'guy,' this 'prehistoric' man, cares what his partner is about and how she feels about the things in her life? Come on!"

Jack tried to find some direction. "Aggie, I really understand your reaction. I get the 'guys are all about themselves' thing. But aren't all the drawings in the messages about what our caveman has learned and is trying to share with his descendants? To me, it looks like he learned that if he first listens, he will better communicate with his partner. That makes so much sense to me."

Peter tries to summarize. "So what I need to understand is that **Communication Starts with Listening?** I don't think I've done a very good job of that. I'm not sure how much more of this I can handle. Let's see what the next message is."

Your Purpose is to Improve the Lives of Everyone in your Life

Drawing shows our man beneath and looking up at the woman, many smaller people, and a hut.

Peter adjusted the lights as everyone positioned themselves.

He shared his interpretation, "Okay, our guy is under every-thing in his life. He has the pressure of taking care of everyone and everything. He has the weight of the world on him, and he obvi-ously feels oppressed because it's all on him. And we know he gets no 'thank you' from anyone. Wow, no thanks, and that's what I saw my father do. Worked two jobs, worked his ass off, and was always tired. We did some weekends of camping and other stuff, but I don't want to sign up for that duty! No thanks, no way!"

Mary saw it differently and contributed her interpretation, "Is our messenger telling us that he sees himself beneath his family and that he is there to lift them up? Is he saying this is what he does and what he is about?"

Ignoring Mary, Aggie added, "You're right, Peter, that's how guys see themselves, punished by the pressure of taking care of every-thing. Give me a break. What about the woman? She's the one doing the cooking, cleaning, and raising all those kids. She's the one doing the heavy lifting. And what's he doing? Hunting and fishing? Cutting down a tree or two? Big deal! That's why guys abandoned their fam-ilies. They can't handle it! You don't think she wouldn't like to go hunting and fishing? You think she would get to? No way. Women can't do that! But he can drag the 'kill' home, and she has to clean it because that's her job, right?"

Jack was moved by this misinterpretation of what men and women do together.

"If that were true, Aggie, there wouldn't be any families. Don't families have a balance that they find? If he's good at the hunting and fishing thing, isn't that what he should be doing? And if she enjoys doing the cooking and being with the kids, isn't that what she wanted to do? Men and women bail because something takes away the rewards of being a wife or a husband, a dad or a mom, and a provider."

"I do understand that, Jack, and I really love that balance," added Mary. "When Alex and I are together, we talk about our fam-ily. When we are with the kids, we take care of them, play with them, we love them, and we love being with them. I am myself, and Alex is himself. We have our roles, and the roles are so natural. It seems like it is why we are here. It is so fulfilling, so rewarding I am overwhelmed right now with how much I miss them, how I am not whole without them. This ancient man, this beautiful man is giving us such a gift. It is a gift of love. Love of his world, his family, and it can't happen if you don't love yourself. It all comes from there, doesn't it?"

Mary paused and then added, "I also think he is showing humility. He is putting the partner and family above himself."

Mary's emotions had warmed everyone as she sat on the nearest stone and surveyed her friends and the messages they had been exposed to. The cavern was filled with the emotion and reflection that Mary had presented for them to consider. Finally, Jack tried to share his take on the drawings and Mary's thoughts.

"I appreciate your feelings very much, Mary. I can only speak for myself, but what you shared is just where I am. I am not a special guy. I am doing what I love, exploring our world and our human history. But it would not be worth doing without my Amy at home. We have raised our kids, and it has been the most wonderful, yes, challenging, adventure a man could ever want. What we are talking about is purpose. Early on I questioned what was going on, why was I doing all this stuff. I didn't make a lot of conscious decisions. I just did what made sense, natural, right, and here I am. I'm in a cavern, exploring these messages with you, loving it, and can't wait to get home.

After a few moments Jack added with a big smile on his face, "Now that I stand back, absorbing this message and our conversation, it reminds me of my favorite movie, *Groundhog Day*! Do you guys know this movie?"

Aggie acknowledged that she did.

"*Groundhog Day*, really? Isn't that where the Bill Murray character gets stuck in some kind of time warp and can't get out of it?"

"That's it, Aggie," affirmed Jack, "but I've always been surprised at how few people understood the message."

Jack sat down to explain the lesson of the movie, "It's the story of a weatherman, Phil Conners, played by Bill Murray, and has to go to Punxsutawney, Pennsylvania, for the Groundhog Day event. He is a self-centered, arrogant jcrk that is locked into a one-day time loop and can't escape. He does everything to end the day. He explores everything that is about him, can't escape, and then tries to kill himself. Finally, he goes a different direction. He becomes about others. He takes everything he has learned about everyone and takes care of all of them. As the story ends, he finds everyone loves him, and he is the happiest he has ever been. That, I think, is the message our benefactor has presented, and it reinforces what I have learned about why we are here. He is telling us his purpose. It's about him, but not about him. He is telling us **Your Purpose is to improve the Lives of Everyone in Your Life**. It is what he does for others that defines him."

This caused Peter to ask the question, "Jack, is that why you asked our waiter in Ankara his name and why you took the time to learn a little about him? I have to tell you that I was very impressed with how positively he reacted to your conversation. Does that connect with what we are talking about here?"

"Peter, I hadn't thought about it that way until now, but I think it does. We made it about him, he was important enough to stop our conversation and ask. We showed him respect. It was about him for just a few minutes, and that is how nearly everyone reacts when I do that. That's why I do it."

Pausing for his colleagues to respond, Jack continued, "Just a few messages ago I mentioned that I learned that we never really find ourselves, but in fact, we define ourselves. I hope you are okay with me going back there. I am convinced he is telling us he found the most important concern he has is his family and their wellbeing. What a wonderful statement, and to think I have the same feelings about my life thousands of years later."

"Jack, I agree," added Mary. "And still the most amazing part of this is he has no other influences. His mind and heart are not full of all the stuff that we hear and see in our world today. And yet here he has explained the most important message he has. He is telling us why we are here."

Legacy, What We Leave Behind

Our final wall drawing depicts our teacher over the message surrounded by little crosses, looking down on many people. Assembled are what looks like his female mate, smaller people, and other layers of more people.

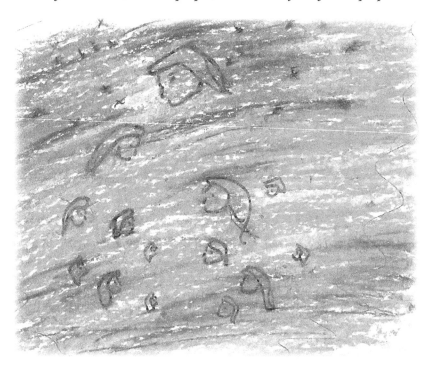

The team settled into their places to see what our teacher had left for them.

Aggie had questions she shared, "Is he looking down now on his woman and the children? Is he 'lording' over them? And what are the little crosses that are all around him?"

Peter pointed to the little crosses surrounding our man and asked, "So what are the crosses about? Are they some kind symbol of where points have 'landed'? I think that's what the little crosses are. What else could they be?"

Our team quietly viewed the final scene. Aggie wanted to share her view. She had come a long way since they entered the cavern.

"If this caveman has done all this and is now looking down on what he has done. He has taken care of this woman and raised a family with her. It looks like he is also showing that he has produced grandchildren and even great-grandchildren. Is that right?"

"Aggie is right," added Jack. "He is displaying his legacy, and he is proud of what he has done. And I think the little crosses are the stars in the heavens. I think he knows this is what he has left behind and that he will be gone someday. I even think he knows there is an afterlife, and he will be able to see his life's work forever. He is telling us eventually, it's about our **Legacy, What we leave Behind**, that we will judge our lives by."

"This is more than I ever dreamed we could find, Jack," confessed Aggie. "I don't know where we are going with all this. I have to think about it. Personally, I have to think about what is going on with my marriage. I now realize that my husband may have given up trying to earn points because I never rewarded him. He didn't have anything to keep track of. I remember now when we were together early on, he always made me laugh, said very nice things to me about how I made him feel, and complimented me all the time. Now I know why he quit. He didn't get anything back."

Peter jumped to his feet and said, "All right, I get it! My 50 percent wasn't even that much, and I haven't been working on how I feel about me, so how could I take care of her? Maybe if we talk about these together, maybe Jasmine and I can get back to where we started. I think I just have to let all this settle."

Mary wanted to support both of her associates. "Aggie, Peter, maybe it's not too late. Maybe knowing all this, you can start over?"

Aggie was looking for direction. "I don't know, Mary, but I think I want to try. Now, what do I do with what we have found and interpreted? I'm overwhelmed, and I'm not sure how the world will use this. Look at the arguments we've had and how twisted our first impressions were."

Nodding in agreement, Jack added, "You're right to be cautious, Aggie. The world is very inside out these days. There doesn't seem to be the respect for the basics, self-respect, gratitude for the people around us, and most importantly, personal responsibility. Who knows how those that are 'insulted' by these ideas will react. Most likely they'll attack each and every one of these messages."

Jack had summarized what each of the team members began to recognize.

Aggie needed to bring this together and to find direction.

"I know you're right, Jack, and it will happen. I heard a long time ago that a lie does not live long enough to grow old. The truth is the truth, and that is what he has left us. I believe what Mary said earlier is the foundation of what we see here. The purity of the message is so important. When I think of all the influences we all have in our world today—so many lies, so many perversions, so many manipulations of the truth—we have to share this."

The group considered Aggie's comments, looked at each other and all the drawings, and finally, Jack attempted to summarize, "Aggie, you're right that the world will have many different reactions, and yes, people will attack it because it's contrary to their values, their biases. Reminds me of what my dad said to me when I was leaving home. He said, 'It was all so different before everything changed.' It will be interesting and maybe some fun to see what nerves this touches."

Aggie seemed very emotional and said, "Jack, speaking just for myself, I so appreciate your patience. I'm a different person standing here and feel very positive for the life I have ahead."

Mary just smiled and listened to the comments and support.

"I can't wait to watch Alex looking at these and hearing how he interprets the drawings. I wonder if he and I will repeat some of the comments that we have had. That might be how many people will walk through this. Maybe we can present this the same way we have seen it."

Peter jumped up with excitement and said, "That's it! Mary has the answer. These messages are simple, and many 'authorities' will try to dissect all of it and three hundred to four hundred pages later, mess the whole thing up. Why don't we publish an easy-to-read, maybe fifty pages, include the drawings exactly as they are, and get this out to the masses! I know all my friends will get it, talk about it, and I'll bet they will love it! I'll even do the first draft!"

As the team lead, Aggie committed to Peter's idea and said, "Peter, I've recorded everything since we walked into this cavern, this wonderful museum. You can take this and put it to print. How much time do you need?"

"Aggie, I can do that in less than a week. Should we meet again to critique before we publish?"

"Yes, and once we put the finishing touches on it, we will call a press conference so that our interpretation is a part of what the world hears. Can we meet in Washington the last Friday of this month, the twenty-ninth? Oh, and bring your partner. This is really about them, isn't it?"

The team shared smiles, hugs, and promises of secrecy until they meet and are ready to publish. They photographed and measured each of the drawings and the cavern. They packed up their gear and headed back across the desert. Their excitement built during their return as they knew the future would be very exciting and could be a different life then what they had before. We will see.

ABOUT THE AUTHOR

Ron Bergstrom, aka R.J., is the oldest of six, and entered the insurance industry in 1978. Many experiences in building his first agency and then in several management roles helped him to understand many different relationships and how they work. R. J. understands the interdependence we have with each other and how to build ourselves, and others in our lives. It is why we are here, and the lessons are concepts we inherently know and can embrace when we understand the basics. R.J. is happily married to Amy, the "girl next door", and they have two beautiful children, Anne and Alex. Amy and R.J. are also blessed with many wonderful friends who, just by how they live their lives, have contributed to this story. R.J. credits these ideas to them having wonderful lives. But it all starts with understanding points.

For more information:
Website   understandingpoints.com
Facebook   Understanding Points
Instagram   Understanding Points

CPSIA information can be obtained
at www.ICGtesting.com
Printed in the USA
LVHW070346290520
656402LV00012BA/504